9 LEADERSHIP LESSONS

From TEA BAG

Build Resilience, Empower Teams and spark Innovation: Create a High-Performance Team Culture for Exceptional Success

GYAN S NARAYAN

CONTENTS

Chapter One: Introduction 5

Chapter Two: Learning Leadership: The Story of David and Michael 13

Chapter Three: What Matters is What's inside the Tea Bag 22

Chapter Four: The real flavor emerges when the tea bag meets hot water 32

Chapter Five: Tea Bag must be porous 41

Chapter Six: Teabags work, never mind where they are in the cup 51

Chapter Seven: Sometimes, one Teabag is just not enough 58

Chapter Eight: Sometimes, you need to add some sugar and milk 65

Chapter Nine: Someone else hold the string always 74

Chapter Ten: It's all about how good tea is. Not the Teabag! 80

Chapter Eleven: Eventually, Teabags need to make way and get out 86

Summary of Book 92

Bonus Chapter of my published book 111

"Grab Your Victory Hour" 111

Bonus Chapter of my published book 129

"Wake Up Your Sleeping Giant" 129

Bonus Chapter of my published book 142

"5 Minutes of Daily Visualization" 142

May I ask you a small favor 162

Acknowledgement 163

Copyright 164

Claim your Gift.

Thanks for Purchasing the Book.

Scan the QR code **to get your free gift.**

Chapter One: Introduction

"The tea bag: it doesn't reveal its true flavor in cold water. It's in hot water—when things get tough—that its best qualities emerge".

We've all heard the saying, "The only constant in life is change." It's a truth I fully embrace. When we say that change is constant, it means that everything around us is continuously evolving—situations, circumstances, ideas, environments, and even our minds. We've all experienced this firsthand. When you walk into your office, things might be different. When you travel, you might notice that the metro station got a fresh coat of paint overnight. Visiting your old school, you see how much the ambience has changed. Even your hometown has transformed with new roads and beautiful gardens. Everywhere you look, change is happening.

Close your eyes and think about all the changes you've witnessed. Often, these changes go unnoticed because we take them for granted. We see the world moving, economies growing, and accept that changes are inevitable. But in this rush, we often miss appreciating these changes. We're so caught up in the flow of life that we forget to consciously live it. Like a boat drifting with the current, we don't steer ourselves to explore different perspectives and experiences.

By consciously embracing and appreciating changes, we can live a life full of joy and learning. Many things in our lives go unnoticed, yet they hold great value. Mother Nature offers endless lessons if we observe closely. From the flight of birds to the resilience of plants, the slow growth of bamboo to the discipline of ants, nature is a treasure trove of wisdom. The rising sun, the flow of waves, the serenity of the moon and stars—all these elements have lessons to teach us.

One everyday item that deeply fascinated me is the tea bag. We use it daily, often without thinking about its qualities. The tea bag's characteristics inspired me to write this book, " 9 Leadership Lessons from Tea Bag." In it, I share nine lessons from the tea bag, blending them with my experiences in the corporate world. These lessons aren't confined to the workplace—they apply to every aspect of life.

Consider the tea bag: it doesn't reveal its true flavor in cold water. It's in hot water—when things get tough—that its best qualities emerge. Similarly, true leadership shines in challenging situations. This book explores how we can learn and grow from these everyday experiences, helping you uncover your true potential.

Each chapter delves into a different aspect of the tea bag's behavior, offering insights that can help you lead a more conscious and fulfilling life. The tea bag teaches us that we reveal our best selves in difficult situations. By reflecting on these lessons, you'll uncover your inherent leadership qualities and learn to face life's challenges with grace and wisdom.

Our actions often stem from principles and beliefs developed over time, but we might not always understand why we behave the way we do. By learning from everyday experiences, like those of a tea bag, we gain clarity and direction. This book will help you see the hidden leader within yourself and guide you in various aspects of life—be it at home, at work, or in social settings.

"9 Leadership Lessons from Tea Bag" is more than just a corporate guide; it's a journey into understanding and appreciating the subtleties of life. By sincerely following the lessons from the tea bag, you'll find yourself growing as an individual and as a leader. The qualities and truths revealed through the tea bag can help you become a better person and uncover the hidden potential within you.

I hope you find joy and value in these lessons. Happy reading!

Summary of Chapter:

The only constant in life is change. This truth is evident everywhere we look—our offices, hometowns, and even our minds are constantly evolving. Yet, we often take these changes for granted, failing to appreciate their significance. By consciously embracing and appreciating change, we can live fuller, more joyful lives. Nature, with its endless lessons from the flight of birds to the growth of bamboo, offers wisdom if we take the time to observe.

One everyday item that inspired me to write this book, "9 Leadership Lessons from Tea Bag," is the humble tea bag. Like a tea bag that reveals its true flavor in hot water, true leadership shines in challenging situations. This book blends lessons from the tea bag with my corporate experiences, offering insights that apply to all aspects of life. Each chapter explores a different aspect of the tea bag's behavior, helping you uncover your leadership potential and face life's challenges with grace and wisdom. This journey is about understanding and appreciating life's subtleties, guiding you to grow as an individual and a leader.

Chapter Two: Learning Leadership: The Story of David and Michael

"I am not afraid of an army of lions led by a sheep; I am afraid of an army of sheep led by a lion"

Let me tell you a story that might make it easier to understand some important facts. As you read, try to picture the characters, and relate them to the corporate world you might have experienced.

There were two friends, David and Michael. They were childhood buddies who studied and played together. Both were equally talented, but David was humble and made friends easily. Michael, on the other hand, was more reserved and a bit arrogant, believing he was smarter than everyone else. He only worked and played on his own terms and didn't easily get along with others. Although Michael got good grades, his attitude was a problem. David, however, excelled in school, always securing the top position in his class, but he remained down-to-earth, playful, and respectful to his teachers. Everyone liked David because of his friendly nature.

As time passed, David and Michael moved up through school and eventually got into reputed business schools. Life is competitive, and sometimes small differences in scores can lead to big differences in opportunities. In the competitive exams, Michael scored slightly higher than David. As a result, Michael got into one of the top business schools, while David attended a second-tier business school. This was the first time the friends had to part ways for their education, though they kept in touch over the phone, meeting only occasionally.

Two years flew by, and it was time for campus placements. Companies came to recruit students from both schools. Fate had an interesting twist for David and Michael. The same company that visited Michael's top business school also came to David's school, looking to fill the same position. Both friends were interviewed separately and, after a rigorous selection process, both received job offers from the company. Coincidentally, they ended up in the same department and the same position within the company. David and Michael were thrilled to see each other again.

David was truly happy to see his childhood friend. Michael, though glad to see David, felt a bit superior because he had an MBA from a more prestigious business school than David.

Michael's arrogance from childhood had only grown, and he believed he deserved the best of everything. He wanted to dominate the company with his prestigious degree, always thinking he was better than others.

Both friends went through twelve months of induction training and were then assigned different roles within the same department. Michael became the Head of Digital Infrastructure, and David became the Head of Digital Operations, both reporting to the Country Head. Each had a team of 20 officials working under them, and their mission was to create a world-class, customer-oriented digital company. The company frequently provided training sessions, both internally and externally, to enhance their skills.

After a year, both David and Michael became experts in their fields. The Country Head reviewed their performance every fortnight. David's team was praised for their excellent teamwork and progress. However, Michael's team was not performing up to the management's expectations. This led to several instances where the Country Head rebuked Michael in front of his team, which was embarrassing for Michael and disheartening for David.

Michael's ego stopped him from accepting advice, even from David. His performance kept getting worse. At the yearly review, David's leadership and his team's success were celebrated, earning them the award for best employee of the year. In contrast, Michael's performance was poor, and his team didn't even meet half of their targets. The management warned Michael to improve within six months or risk being fired.

This was a huge blow to Michael. His arrogance had led to a decline in team morale and performance. David, seeing his friend struggle, couldn't stay silent. He approached Michael and offered to help. Initially resistant, Michael eventually accepted David's advice, knowing his job was on the line.

David took Michael to a quiet boardroom and asked him about his working style, team dynamics, and approach. After a long conversation, David identified the issues. He wanted to share a valuable leadership lesson he had learned from something as simple as a tea bag.

David ordered two cups of tea. The office boy brought hot water, tea bags, milk, sugar, and a spoon. Michael was confused about what David was trying to show him. David asked his friend to patiently watch and listen to what he was going to do with the tea bag.

With this background, let's dive into the journey of learning leadership lessons from a tea bag. I want my readers to feel comfortable as we get straight to the point. There are nine leadership lessons from a tea bag, and I have dedicated a chapter to each one so you can deeply understand and relate to these lessons in your own life.

Summary of Chapter

David and Michael, childhood friends who took different paths in life, ended up working for the same company. David was humble and approachable, making him well-liked, while Michael was arrogant and isolated, believing in his superiority. Despite both being talented, their attitudes shaped their professional journeys differently. Michael's prestigious MBA degree made him feel entitled and led to a domineering attitude at work, which eventually caused his team's performance to suffer. Meanwhile, David's leadership and teamwork earned his team accolades and recognition.

When Michael's job was on the line due to poor performance, David stepped in to help. Through a simple but powerful demonstration involving a tea bag, David aimed to teach Michael valuable leadership lessons. This story sets the stage for exploring nine leadership lessons drawn from the humble tea bag, emphasizing humility, teamwork, and the importance of staying grounded. These lessons, illustrated through David and Michael's experiences, offer insights applicable to anyone striving to become a better leader and person.

Chapter Three: What Matters is What's inside the Tea Bag
(Leadership Lesson 1)

"The strength of a tea bag isn't in its packaging but in the quality of the tea within. The same goes for leaders."

After a deep conversation with Michael, David discovered that Michael's team was knowledgeable and experienced. They had the capacity to turn the wheels, but somehow the output was missing. There was a lack of team spirit. As David delved deeper, he realized that Michael relied too much on his professional qualification from a reputed business school. Michael felt superior and believed his team members lagged in knowledge and accomplishment. Despite the team's expertise, their approach to problem-solving was often rebuked. They were never encouraged, and internal review meetings led by Michael every morning were a bloodbath for his team. This attitude demotivated them, leading to a decline in performance.

In contrast, David noticed his team was always in high spirits, taking the initiative to come up with solutions. They put their minds and souls into their work. As a result, many of their projects met target dates. This success was because David gave his team a free hand and always appreciated their good work, even if it was a small success. In review meetings, he recognized his team members and shared the organization's vision. He communicated the commitments made to his superiors regarding project deadlines. David monitored the project as a team lead but with humility, believing that all his team members were equally responsible and had the drive to meet targets. He guided his team but never took them for granted or rebuked them. He learned one important lesson, which he always implemented: "Praise in the group but correct in private."

David wanted his friend to understand where his weaknesses lay and how improving them could lead to much better performance. He knew that the truth might be painful, but sometimes it's essential to hold up a mirror to reveal one's mistakes clearly.

David got straight to the point and told his friend to look at a tea bag, asking if he could find any meaning or lessons from it. Michael was clueless and surrendered himself to David, ready to learn the lessons from the tea bag. With this, David began his first lesson.

"What Matters is What's inside the Tea Bag".

The taste of tea is not dependent on the label of the tea bag or the beautiful cover pouch. What matters the taste is the quality of tea inside the tea bag. All teabags come in different types of packaging. Some look fancy, and some look simple. But what really matters is the tea inside the bag, not the packaging. The same is true for people. It doesn't matter what your title is, where you went to school, the clothes you wear, or any other outward appearance. What really counts is who you are inside— your beliefs and attitude. Focus on being a good person, fixing your attitude, and getting your values right. Don't worry about the small stuff. What truly makes a difference is who you are at your core.

The above lessons revealed by David were an eye-opener for Michael as he realized the mistakes he was making and what he was harping on. He recognized that he was always carrying his MBA degree from one of the top business schools in his head, leading to a superiority complex and arrogance. He was not treating his subordinates with the right team spirit.

With this mindset his MBA degree was just a professional certificate that wasn't producing practical results. He realized that he had to change his mindset and keep his team in high spirits for good results. He acknowledged that he never appreciated his team because of his feeling of superiority, believing his team members were there to follow his orders. He realized this approach never works.

Michael could clearly relate to the success of his friend David, who, despite having an MBA degree from a second-tier business school, met all targets. David's team was always motivated and ready to work beyond normal hours. David's leadership was charismatic, and with his team-caring attitude, he won the hearts of his team members. With his knowledge of work, he guided his team efficiently, and overall, all team members, including David, learned from each other and progressed. David's winning mantra was his deep commitment to having a motivated team, maintaining a good mindset, treating everyone equally, and being approachable to his team members. Whenever his team members made mistakes, he corrected them in private and never rebuked them in public.

With the above example, we too have a learning: our qualifications, various professional certificates, our name, and our material possessions do not matter. What matters is who we are at the core and what values we carry. As good human beings, we can always win the hearts of everyone around us and also be at peace with ourselves. With this approach, we can get much better work from our team.

Summary of Chapter

After a deep conversation with Michael, David discovered that Michael's team had the knowledge and experience needed for success, but their output was lacking due to poor team spirit. Michael, relying heavily on his prestigious business school background, felt superior and believed his team members were less knowledgeable. His constant rebukes during morning meetings demotivated his team, leading to a decline in performance. In contrast, David's team thrived because he appreciated their efforts, encouraged initiative, and fostered a positive environment. He believed in recognizing successes publicly and addressing issues privately, which boosted team morale and productivity.

David wanted Michael to understand his shortcomings and how improving his approach could enhance performance. Using the metaphor of a tea bag, David taught Michael that what matters is what's inside— the quality of the tea, not the packaging. Similarly, in leadership, it's not about titles, education, or outward appearances but about one's core values and attitude. Michael realized his mistake of valuing his MBA degree over the team's collective effort and the importance of maintaining a humble and supportive leadership style.

Michael acknowledged that his arrogance and lack of appreciation for his team were detrimental. Inspired by David's success, he saw the importance of motivating his team, treating everyone equally, and being approachable. David's leadership, characterized by humility and a team-caring attitude, resulted in high team morale and consistent success. The lesson is clear: true leadership is about who we are at our core and the values we uphold. By focusing on being good human beings and supporting our teams, we can achieve better results and foster a harmonious work environment.

Chapter Four: The real flavor emerges when the tea bag meets hot water
(Leadership Lesson 2)

"Leadership is like a tea bag; its value is realized only when immersed in hot water, revealing its true essence."

Further interrogation with Michael revealed that many times, if his Country Head gave him a challenging assignment, he would find reasons to escape the responsibility. Michael had a mental block where he wanted to remain confined to his KRA only. He did not want to touch any assignment beyond his allocated role. There was one such incident where the Country Head wanted Michael to prepare a detailed paper on the digital infrastructure of peer companies and adopt the best practices. He also wanted to get the blueprint of the architecture approved by top management in the next Board meeting and, after approval, implement it in the organization within 90 days. The work assigned was challenging and rewarding.

Though the work expected of Michael was a bit of a deviation from his assigned responsibility, as data collection and analysis were the job of the analytics team, the Country Head wanted Michael to complete it to place the agenda in the ensuing Board meeting. The analytics team would have taken more time, and the output might not have aligned with the implementation plan. When the Country Head asked Michael to take the assignment and produce a solid report, Michael did not show much excitement. He feared failing in such a critical and time-bound project. These thoughts discouraged Michael from stepping up and accepting the project. He conveyed his inability to take the assignment, which shocked his Country Head. The Country Head never expected Michael to behave so cowardly, revealing his true colors. His boss felt he had recruited the wrong person, despite Michael's degree from one of the best business schools.

This revelation by Michael to David explained why the Country Head was not happy with Michael and why he received low marks in his annual appraisals. Then, David unfolded the second lesson he had learned from the tea bag – **"The real flavor emerges when the tea bag meets hot water."**

The real flavor emerges when the tea bag meets hot water means that the true essence and strength of the tea only come out when the tea bag is placed in hot water. Lukewarm water won't extract the full flavor and richness of the tea leaves. The heat is necessary to release the tea's true taste and aroma.

This can be seen as a metaphor for people, especially leaders. Just as tea shows its real flavor in hot water, a person's true character and abilities are revealed when they face difficult and challenging situations. When everything is easy and comfortable, you might not see what someone is truly capable of. But under pressure and in tough times, their true strengths, skills, and qualities become apparent. So, just as hot water is essential for brewing strong tea, challenging situations are essential for revealing the true character of a leader.

When things get hard, good leaders get excited because they know it's their time to shine. Challenges give them a chance to prove their worth. So, when you face a difficult situation, think like a tea bag and embrace it. Don't let the fear of failure stop you. It might be your best chance to show what you can really do.

With the above learnings, Michael had an "aha" moment where he realized his mistake. He recognized that he had an opportunity to prove his mettle as a true leader, but he ran away from the responsibility. He could have accepted the challenge, conveyed the project to his team members, and divided the responsibility among them. He could have easily guided and monitored the project for timely completion and meeting the target date. In the corporate sector, your bosses judge you not by your mere knowledge but by how much leadership quality you display. The organization always promotes leaders because leaders turn the wheel and take the organization forward. This learning from the tea bag applies to anyone in any situation. If you want to be a leader in your field, you have to dive into the hot water, and only then will your true colors and leadership qualities emerge.

Summary of Chapter

During a deeper conversation, David learned that Michael often avoided challenging assignments given by his Country Head. Michael preferred to stick to his defined responsibilities and avoid any extra tasks. One incident highlighted this behavior: the Country Head asked Michael to prepare a detailed report on peer companies' digital infrastructure and implement the best practices within 90 days. Although this task was slightly outside Michael's usual duties, it was critical and time-sensitive. Instead of embracing the challenge, Michael declined, fearing failure. This reaction disappointed his Country Head and explained Michael's poor annual appraisals.

David used this revelation to teach Michael a crucial lesson: "The real flavor emerges when the tea bag meets hot water." This metaphor means that just as a tea bag's true flavor is released in hot water, a person's true abilities are revealed in challenging situations. Comfort and ease don't showcase a leader's strengths; adversity does. Good leaders embrace tough times as opportunities to prove their worth. David encouraged Michael to see challenges as chances to demonstrate his leadership qualities rather than shy away from them.

Michael had an "aha" moment, realizing he missed an opportunity to prove himself as a true leader. He understood that he could have accepted the challenge, delegated tasks to his team, and guided the project to success. In the corporate world, leadership qualities, not just knowledge, are what lead to success and recognition. This lesson from the tea bag applies universally: to be a leader, you must embrace challenges and let your true capabilities shine.

Chapter Five: Tea Bag must be porous
(Leadership Lesson 3)

"A true leader infuses their team with wisdom and support, much like a tea bag infuses water with flavor."

The deep discussion with Michael further revealed that his team was not happy and did not contribute on their own unless asked. There was no team spirit or sense of belonging. The team did what was asked and then remained confined to their desks. David thought that something must be wrong with the leader. Perhaps Michael was not open or approachable to his team members. Everyone remained confined in their watertight compartments, with no infusion of knowledge from leader to team members. This clearly indicated a lack of guidance and an expectation of the best from the team without providing support, leading to the team's downfall. As a leader, it is his responsibility to guide team members and share his learnings and experiences with them. David found this missing in Michael's team, and it is a prerequisite for good team spirit.

On the other hand, David's team was always jubilant and ready to share their views, increasing the group's productivity. David ensured to guide his team with his knowledge and experience. He was always approachable and infused his wisdom so that the team received the right inputs to move forward. David believed that his team's victory was his victory and worked closely with them. Many times, he offered ideas when the team got stuck and regularly encouraged brainstorming sessions. He encouraged his team members to attend workshops related to their key areas of work, gain knowledge, and implement it. In a nutshell, David was totally approachable and made a habit of mixing with his teammates. He believed in collaborative working with his guidance wherever required.

David, inspired by his previous insights from Michael, decided to share another valuable lesson on leadership, using the metaphor of a tea bag. He told Michael, "There's another important life lesson you can learn from a tea bag. Remember, **"a teabag must be porous**."

Imagine you have the best tea in the world, and you put it into a bag that's impermeable. It won't work. You just won't be able to make a cup of tea. For teabag to work, it needs to be porous. You need the tea and the water to come in contact with each other.

In our lives too, we cannot survive and thrive in isolation. Leaders need to be careful not to build walls around themselves that prevent people from reaching out to them. As a leader, you need to be able to touch other people. Else, all that's inside will be wasted- untouched by all the good around you. The tea was meant to mix with the water. Similarly, all of us were designed to work with other people, with teams, and with society at large.

David explained further, just like a tea bag needs to be porous to let the water flow through and release its flavor, a good leader must be open and receptive. Being porous means being open to new ideas, feedback, and the experiences of others. It allows you to absorb wisdom from various sources and adapt to different situations. This openness is crucial for personal growth and effective leadership. It helps you connect with your team, understand their needs, and inspire them to achieve their best.

He continued, in life and leadership, being rigid and closed off can limit your potential. Embrace the qualities of a porous tea bag – be adaptable, listen actively, and always be ready to learn and grow. This way, you'll not only enhance your own abilities but also create a more dynamic and harmonious environment for those around you.

The above lesson was a revelation for Michael. He realized where he had been going wrong and why his team wasn't performing well. He recalled many instances where his team needed his support and input to move the project forward, but he didn't step in to provide solutions. This caused delays, with the team often stuck for days or weeks, trying to find a solution through their brainstorming sessions.

Lacking experience, they were looking to their leader for guidance, but Michael didn't believe in being open and sharing his knowledge and experience. He was like the hard, impermeable cover of a tea bag that wouldn't mix with the water. All his knowledge stayed confined within his own tea bag, and despite being a leader with rich experience, his expertise didn't blend with the team's efforts. Consequently, no tea was ever made, and everyone worked in isolation. This was a major reason for his team's failure and why Michael faced awkward situations with his boss.

So, there's a key lesson here for us: as leaders, we must blend with our team and offer full support whenever they need it. This will instill confidence in them and create a cohesive team. Such a team will always be favored by top management. By adopting a porous attitude, you'll not only become a better person but also gain appreciation from your superiors. In the process, you'll set an example for others to follow.

Summary of Chapter

During a deep discussion, David realized that Michael's team lacked motivation and did not take the initiative unless explicitly directed. There was no team spirit or sense of belonging. Michael's leadership style was unapproachable, leading to a lack of guidance and support. As a result, the team felt isolated and unmotivated, contributing to their poor performance. In contrast, David's team thrived because he was open, approachable, and regularly shared his knowledge and experiences. This fostered a collaborative environment where team members felt valued and encouraged to contribute, significantly boosting productivity.

David used the metaphor of a tea bag to teach Michael an important lesson about leadership. He explained that just as a tea bag needs to be porous to release its flavor, a leader must be open and receptive. This means being open to new ideas, feedback, and the experiences of others. By doing so, a leader can absorb wisdom from various sources and adapt to different situations, promoting personal growth and effective leadership. This openness helps leaders connect with their teams, understand their needs, and inspire them to achieve their best.

Michael had an "aha" moment, realizing his mistake of isolating himself and not providing the necessary support to his team. He understood that being closed off had limited his team's potential and caused delays in their projects. Michael learned that by being more open and supportive, he could instill confidence in his team, creating a cohesive and high-performing group. This lesson taught him that blending with his team and adopting a porous attitude would not only improve his leadership but also gain appreciation from his superiors and set a positive example for others.

Chapter Six: Teabags work, never mind where they are in the cup
(Leadership Lesson 4)

"True leaders, like teabags, make an impact regardless of their position within the organization."

The dialogue between David and Michael continued, with David seeking to understand Michael's pain points while Michael spoke from the heart to get advice from his friend. Through their conversation, David discovered that Michael was an autocratic leader who did not motivate his subordinates. Michael believed that his team was there to follow his orders and execute tasks as directed. He saw them as helpers in his job, considering the entire project his responsibility. His team was there to work at his command, and he didn't allow them to share ideas or innovate. In essence, he was stifling the creativity and potential of his coworkers. David realized that this attitude was detrimental to both Michael's progress and that of his team. By not recognizing and nurturing his team's talent, Michael was missing out on valuable contributions that could turn a project around.

Seeing this, David felt compelled to tell Michael that he was stifling the leadership qualities of his team members. With genuine concern, David told his friend, "You are making a big mistake with your teammates and killing the leadership in them." Michael was taken aback and wanted to know what David meant. He argued that as the leader, his team members were there to take orders from him, believing that a team could only have one leader. Understanding his friend's mindset, David knew it was time to correct Michael's perspective. He shared another lesson from the tea bag metaphor, saying, **"Teabags work, never mind where they are in the cup."**

Once you place a teabag in a cup, its position doesn't affect its function. Whether it's at the top, side, or bottom, it will still brew effectively. The idea that leadership is confined to the person at the top of an organization is a misconception.

Leaders exist at every level, and your place in the hierarchy shouldn't constrain your leadership potential. True leaders draw their strength from within, not from their title or position. Great leaders understand

this and seek out leadership qualities in every corner of the organization.

David explained to his friend that it is a mistaken notion that leadership is only about the person at the top of the organization. Leaders are everywhere. You shouldn't let your 'position' in the hierarchy limit your impact as a leader. Position is irrelevant. Leaders derive their strength from within, not from a title or position in the organization. Truly great leaders recognize this. They look for leaders in every corner of the organization.

This realization was an eye-opener for Michael. He recognized the mistake he had been making with his team. Though surrounded by talented individuals, he had always believed he was the only one capable of achieving success. Michael realized that each team member was a leader, and their designations didn't matter. Just like a tea bag infuses the same taste and aroma regardless of where it's placed in the cup, his team members could contribute their skills and leadership qualities regardless of their titles.

He understood that every individual, even those at the bottom of the organizational pyramid, could bring valuable contributions and foster a positive atmosphere within the team. This, in turn, would elevate the organization to greater heights. Michael realized that ideas could come from anyone and that all his teammates possessed leadership qualities. As the leader of his department, he felt it was his duty to nurture these qualities and help his team members realize their potential.

Summary of Chapter

David and Michael's conversation revealed that Michael's autocratic leadership style stifled his team's creativity and potential. Michael saw his team merely as helpers to follow his orders, which hindered their ability to share ideas or innovate. David recognized this attitude was harmful to both Michael and his team. He explained to Michael that leadership isn't confined to a position at the top; true leaders can be found at every level of an organization.

Using the tea bag metaphor, David highlighted that a tea bag functions no matter where it is in the cup, just as leadership potential isn't limited by hierarchy. This eye-opening lesson made Michael realize his mistake. He understood that every team member has leadership qualities, and it's crucial to nurture and encourage these qualities to elevate the entire organization. Michael resolved to support his team better and recognize their contributions, fostering a positive and collaborative atmosphere

Chapter Seven: Sometimes, one Teabag is just not enough

(Leadership Lesson 5)

"Great leaders recognize that sometimes, one person's efforts aren't enough; true success comes from collaborating and leveraging the strengths of the whole team."

With the previous lessons, Michael was very happy as David kept sharing insights that opened his mind. Each lesson had a great impact, making Michael feel ready to excel in his organization. But there were still many lessons to learn, and Michael was eager to hear more from his friend.

The discussions between David and Michael continued, and David observed that Michael was trying to take on all the work alone, even though it wasn't possible for one person to complete it all. Michael had committed to the top management to finish the project by himself within the scheduled time but always failed to deliver. It became clear that Michael was overwhelmed by the workload. He believed he could handle the project alone and, as a hard taskmaster, made his team work day and night. This assumption led him to failure. Both Michael and his organization suffered because of it. The project was time-sensitive and challenging, causing Michael and his team to stay late in the office long after everyone else had left. Michael wanted to handle everything himself, hoping to roll out the project and earn appreciation and promotion. Despite feeling the need for support from other leaders to share the workload and discuss speeding up the project, he never involved his colleagues, wanting to be a one-man army. Understanding Michael's mindset, David told him that his approach was harmful to both him and the organization. David felt it was time to share the next lesson from the tea bag, which perfectly addressed Michael's mindset - "**Sometimes, one Teabag is just not enough**".

If the pot is very large, one teabag may not be enough to make a good beverage. Despite its best effort, the tea won't be strong enough. The simple solution is to add another teabag.

This idea applies to organizations too. Sometimes, the size of the challenge requires more than one leader. Leaders shouldn't feel inadequate or incompetent when asking for help. Too often, good leaders are branded as failures—not because they weren't capable, but because the challenge was too big for one person. Asking for assistance is not a sign of weakness; it is often a sign of great strength and self-confidence.

The above lesson was an eye-opener for Michael. He realized that while he often thought about seeking help from his colleagues, he never acted on it. He wanted to complete the project alone to impress top management. But today, he understood that this mindset was the main reason for his failure. The lessons from the tea bag were so clear that they didn't need further explanation. It was an enlightenment for Michael, revealing the mistakes he had been making for years. He thought he should have approached his boss to discuss the project's enormity and timelines. He could have asked for a colleague's support to drive the project to completion. This approach would have led to the organization's success, and he would have been appreciated for his leadership. It would have been a win-win situation for him.

Summary of Chapter

Michael was very happy with the previous lessons as David's insights opened his mind, making him feel ready to excel in his organization. However, there were still more lessons to learn, and Michael was eager to hear them. David noticed that Michael was trying to handle all the work alone, committing to finishing projects by himself but failing to deliver. Overwhelmed by the workload, Michael's assumption that he could manage everything alone led to failure, causing both him and his organization to suffer. Despite needing support, Michael never involved his colleagues, aiming to be a one-man army. David saw this mindset as harmful and shared the lesson, "Sometimes, one teabag is just not enough."

David explained that just as a large pot of tea needs more than one teabag to make a strong beverage, big challenges in an organization often require more than one leader. Asking for help is not a sign of weakness but a sign of strength and self-confidence. This lesson was an eye-opener for Michael. He realized that his failure to seek help was the main reason for his struggles. Understanding this, Michael acknowledged that he should have approached his boss and colleagues for support, which would have led to success and appreciation for his leadership. This change in mindset was crucial for Michael's growth and the overall success of the organization.

Chapter Eight: Sometimes, you need to add some sugar and milk
(Leadership Lesson 6)

"Effective leadership often requires adding the right mix of support and resources to bring out the best in your team."

Michael felt increasingly confident as he absorbed valuable lessons from his friend David. These insights were changing his mindset, and he was ready to transform himself. Eager to learn more, he humbly asked David if there were still few more lessons from the tea bag that could help him improve. David was thrilled to see his friend's enthusiasm and felt fulfilled knowing he was positively impacting Michael's life. They continued their conversation, delving deeper into Michael's mistakes with his team that led to failure.

David learned that Michael's project required expertise in areas like analytics, Management Information Systems, and Information Technology. For the project to succeed, it needed input from these critical fields, which were outside Michael's expertise. Michael had some ideas but wasn't an expert. He had the attitude of a one-man army, wanting to take all the credit for the project. He feared that involving colleagues from other departments would undermine his recognition.

Because of this mindset, Michael took full responsibility for the project and didn't allow any intervention from his colleagues. David was shocked to learn this and realized

Michael's approach was leading to disaster, not only for himself but for the organization. Michael's attempt to complete the project alone, without input from essential departments, was unacceptable to David. He couldn't control his emotions and saw Michael's attitude as selfish, aiming for personal achievement at the cost of the organization's success.

David knew that even if the project succeeded in the short term, it would eventually fail without strong foundational support, impacting the organization more than Michael. Feeling suffocated by the situation, David knew it was time for Michael to learn a new lesson from the tea bag, perfectly suited to address his current mindset – **"Sometimes, you need to add some sugar and milk"**.

Sometimes, you need to add some sugar and milk. If you're looking for a cup of tea with milk and sugar, a teabag alone won't do the trick. You need to add the milk and sugar yourself to get the desired taste.

Similarly, in business, no single leader can possess every necessary skill. Good leaders understand this and seek out partners or colleagues who have complementary skills. They work together to fill in the gaps.

By collaborating with others, leaders ensure that the final result meets the objective. This teamwork is like adding sugar and milk to tea, creating a well-rounded and satisfying outcome.

The above lesson was an eye-opener for Michael as he realized the mistakes he had been making for the sake of personal recognition. Michael was an expert in digital operations but lacked deep knowledge in analytics, Management Information Systems, and Information Technology. To prove he could handle the entire project alone, he didn't seek help from his boss to involve colleagues from other departments who were experts in these areas.

Michael tried to gather knowledge by reading books and reference materials, working round the clock and bringing stress upon himself. This not only exhausted him but also forced his team to stay late in the office, often without having tasks to complete, leading to their displeasure.

Despite his efforts, the project didn't progress as expected. Michael often got stuck and relied on circulars and reference materials to resolve issues, which delayed the project and harmed the organization.

With the above lessons from the tea bag, Michael realized he could have approached his boss to request experts for the project when needed. This would have solved his problems and saved hours for himself and his team. He could have focused solely on the project's outcome and been stress-free.

This lesson is true for all of us. As project leaders, we shouldn't take all the burden on ourselves. Instead, we should involve experts from other domains as needed to ensure the right inputs are in place and the project rollout is seamless.

Summary of Chapter

Michael felt increasingly confident as he absorbed valuable lessons from his friend David. Eager to improve, he humbly asked David if there were more lessons from the tea bag to learn. David was thrilled by Michael's enthusiasm and felt fulfilled knowing he was making a positive impact. As their conversation continued, David discovered that Michael's project needed expertise in areas like analytics, Management Information Systems, and Information Technology. Michael, wanting all the credit, feared that involving colleagues would undermine his recognition. This mindset led him to take full responsibility and avoid seeking help, which David saw as a recipe for disaster.

David explained that just as adding sugar and milk to tea enhances its flavor, leaders need to collaborate with colleagues who have complementary skills. Michael's attempt to handle the project alone resulted in delays and dissatisfaction among his team, as he worked round the clock, causing unnecessary stress. The project failed to progress as expected because Michael relied solely on his limited knowledge and didn't seek the necessary expertise from others. David emphasized that good leaders understand their limitations and seek help to achieve a well-rounded outcome.

The lesson was an eye-opener for Michael. He realized that seeking help from colleagues would have solved many problems, saved time, and reduced stress for both him and his team. This insight applies to all of us: as project leaders, we shouldn't bear all the burden alone. Involving experts from different domains ensures that the right inputs are in place and the project rollout is seamless, leading to successful outcomes and a more harmonious work environment.

Chapter Nine: Someone else hold the string always

(Leadership Lesson 7)

"True leaders remain humble, always remembering that their power and influence are ultimately held by those they serve and answer to."

Through their conversations, David noticed many issues with Michael's attitude toward his team and his work style. He sensed that Michael was arrogant and tried to do everything himself. David felt it was time to wrap up the lessons but wanted to share one final, crucial teaching from the tea bag metaphor. This lesson wasn't just for the moment but a principle for Michael to remember and stay grounded in his work. David continued his teachings, pointing to the tea bag in the cup as he explained- **"Someone else hold the string always"**.

No matter how strong the teabag is, it recognizes that someone else holds the string in his or her hands. And they can pull the teabag out and throw it away anytime they like. No questions asked. That's a humbling thought which leaders must never lose sight of. No matter how powerful a leader becomes, he must remember there is a string tied to him that's in the hand of some other stakeholder or the board- or just some other more powerful force. The realization of this truth can help ensure that leaders don't let power go to their head and

begin seeing themselves as lords and masters of all.

Michael understood what his friend was trying to say but wanted to delve deeper. At Michael's request, David explained further. He said that no matter what position a leader holds, they shouldn't act like the owner. As a leader, you are responsible for guiding the project to success, but once it's live, you shouldn't cling to it as if it solely belongs to you.

Believing you own the project can lead to an autocratic style, rejecting any interference. You start guarding your project jealously, making every decision alone, and forcefully pushing your ideas to top management. This attitude can irritate the management and backfire. They might react negatively to your behavior, potentially leading to your removal from the position.

The key lesson is to always stay grounded and humble in your work. As a leader, your role is to guide the team and ensure the project is on the right track. You should be a doer, not an owner. Remember, in an organization, your top bosses are always watching. You have the freedom to manage your assigned tasks, but your goal is to contribute to the organization's success. You are not the ultimate boss. If you overstep, just like a tea bag with a string, your bosses can pull you out. The tea bag's job is to make good tea, but it can't claim the cup forever. Once the tea is made, someone else pulls it out by the string.

These insights from the tea bag metaphor were clear to Michael, and he felt enlightened by his friend's wisdom.

Summary of chapter

Through their conversations, David noticed Michael's arrogance and tendency to do everything himself. David decided to share one final lesson from the tea bag metaphor to help Michael stay grounded. He explained that just as a tea bag has a string held by someone else, leaders must remember they are accountable to others. No matter how powerful a leader becomes, there are always stakeholders or higher authorities who can pull them out of their position. This realization helps prevent leaders from becoming autocratic and ensures they remain humble.

Michael understood the importance of this lesson. He learned that as a leader, his role is to guide the team and ensure the project's success without becoming possessive or authoritarian. Acting like the sole owner of a project can lead to negative consequences and potentially result in removal from the position. The key is to stay grounded, humble, and focused on contributing to the organization's success, recognizing that ultimate control lies with higher authorities. These insights helped Michael see the value of humility and accountability in leadership.

Chapter Ten: It's all about how good tea is. Not the Teabag!
(Leadership Lesson 8)

"Great leadership is measured by the success of the team, not by individual accolades."

In this lesson, David wanted Michael to grasp a crucial insight from the tea bag metaphor. He explained that the teaching which he was going to impart was like the tabletop, resting on the four legs. Without delay, David began by telling his friend that a leader's primary goal should be to build a strong team, focusing less on themselves and more on their team's development.

Michael didn't fully understand the deep meaning behind David's words and asked for further clarification. Without much hesitation, David shared another lesson from the tea bag metaphor with Michael- **It's all about how good the tea is. Not the Teabag!**

No one ever drinks a cup of tea and exclaims, 'What an amazing tea bag!' Instead, they say, 'That was a fantastic cup of tea!' In the ultimate analysis, leaders are remembered not for their individual brilliance but for the excellence of their teams and the enduring institutions they build. All too often, leaders become focused with their own reflections, forgetting to shine the spotlight on their teams, organizations, and results. Great leaders understand this fundamental

truth: 'It's not about me. It's about them.'

The lesson was clear. Leadership isn't about self-focus or boasting about personal achievements. Often, leaders forget that their success comes from their team members, who deserve more credit. Unfortunately, it's common for leaders to ignore their teams' contributions when they achieve a goal, presenting the success as their own.

What leaders fail to realize is that bosses and others are aware of the efforts and contributions of the entire team. Just like when people enjoy a cup of tea, they praise the tea itself, not the tea bag. Similarly, people appreciate the final result of a project without focusing on the individual leader behind it. They see the work as a whole and value the overall outcome.

When we admire great monuments, technological innovations, or high-rise buildings, we appreciate the work and effort behind them, not just the project leader. This applies to leaders in any organization. They shouldn't be attached to the outcome or seek individual praise once a project is completed.

A good leader ensures that the people behind the scenes are recognized and appreciated. This mindset helps leaders grow within the organization, and top management notices those who care for their team without seeking self-publicity. Leaders who demonstrate this care and humility are the ones who get promoted and climb the corporate ladder seamlessly.

Summary of Chapter

David wanted Michael to understand a crucial insight from the tea bag metaphor: a leader's primary goal should be to build a strong team, focusing less on themselves and more on their team's development. He explained that no one praises the tea bag itself but the quality of the tea it produces. Similarly, great leaders are remembered not for their individual brilliance but for the success and excellence of their teams.

Michael learned that leadership isn't about self-focus or boasting about personal achievements. Often, leaders forget that their success is due to their team's efforts, and they should shine the spotlight on their team's contributions. Just like people appreciate the tea and not the tea bag, successful projects are valued for the collective effort rather than the individual leader. A good leader recognizes and appreciates the people behind the scenes, which helps them grow within the organization. Leaders who demonstrate care and humility are the ones who get promoted and advance seamlessly up the corporate ladder.

Chapter Eleven: Eventually, Teabags need to make way and get out
(Leadership Lesson 9)

"True leaders know when to step aside, allowing others to shine and the organization to thrive."

Everyone in an organization is on a conveyor belt that's always moving. Eventually, every person will exit, whether from the organization or a project they've worked on passionately. David wanted Michael to clearly understand this final lesson. No one is indispensable. Some people think if they start a project, it belongs to them for as long as they're there. They dislike interference and want to keep control forever. But this isn't correct; every project is a time-bound exercise.

There's an initial setup period, a nurturing phase, and then the results. Once the project is producing results and runs smoothly, it becomes a regular activity with established systems and procedures. At this point, when the project is fully matured, it's time for the leader to exit. The leader should share their knowledge with the next person and move on, whether to a different department or a new project, as needed by the organization.

The key point David wanted to convey to Michael was that once his role as a project leader is done, he should move on. He shouldn't cling to the project. Eager to understand this final lesson deeply, Michael listened as David shared the last wisdom from the humble tea bag- **Eventually, Teabags need to make way and get out.**

Teabags know that once the tea is brewed, it's time to move on. They don't worry about leaving the cup because they understand that staying longer would get in the way of someone enjoying their tea. Unfortunately, many leaders think they are indispensable and overstay their welcome. They become so convinced of their own importance that they believe the organization can't survive without them. They get too attached to their role and the organization and don't want to leave. So, think of the teabag. Remember that leaving is a normal and necessary part of the process.

The above lesson from the tea bag was now crystal clear to Michael. He thoroughly understood its essence and felt greatly relieved. Reflecting on the nine leadership lessons he learned from the tea bag, Michael felt enlightened. He was deeply grateful to his friend David, who had been a savior in his life, providing him with invaluable wisdom.

Michael was ready for a change. He knew he needed to transform into the kind of leader who truly cares for his team and understands the importance of growing together. With a fresh perspective and renewed determination, Michael decided to show his boss the new him. He planned to ask for six months to turn the project around, confident that he could apply the valuable lessons he learned from the simple, yet profound, example of a tea bag.

Summary of Chapter

David wanted Michael to understand a crucial lesson: no one in an organization is indispensable. Every person, no matter how passionate, will eventually leave the project or the company. David explained that projects have distinct phases: setup, nurturing, and then producing results. Once a project is running smoothly, it becomes a routine activity, and it's time for the leader to move on. Leaders should share their knowledge and let others take over to keep the organization growing.

Using the tea bag metaphor, David emphasized that just as tea bags know when to leave the cup after brewing, leaders should know when to step aside. Overstaying and clinging to their role can hinder progress. Michael understood this clearly and felt relieved. Grateful for David's wisdom, he pledged to revive his project with a new approach.

Summary of Book

Chapter One

The only constant in life is change. This truth is evident everywhere we look—our offices, hometowns, and even our minds are constantly evolving. Yet, we often take these changes for granted, failing to appreciate their significance. By consciously embracing and appreciating change, we can live fuller, more joyful lives. Nature, with its endless lessons from the flight of birds to the growth of bamboo, offers wisdom if we take the time to observe.

One everyday item that inspired me to write this book, "9 Leadership Lessons from Tea Bag," is the humble tea bag. Like a tea bag that reveals its true flavor in hot water, true leadership shines in challenging situations. This book blends lessons from the tea bag with my corporate experiences, offering insights that apply to all aspects of life. Each chapter explores a different aspect of the tea bag's behavior, helping you uncover your leadership potential and face life's challenges with grace and wisdom. This journey is about understanding and appreciating life's subtleties, guiding you to grow as an individual and a leader.

Chapter Two

David and Michael, childhood friends who took different paths in life, ended up working for the same company. David was humble and approachable, making him well-liked, while Michael was arrogant and isolated, believing in his superiority. Despite both being talented, their attitudes shaped their professional journeys differently. Michael's prestigious MBA degree made him feel entitled and led to a domineering attitude at work, which eventually caused his team's performance to suffer. Meanwhile, David's leadership and teamwork earned his team accolades and recognition.

When Michael's job was on the line due to poor performance, David stepped in to help. Through a simple but powerful demonstration involving a tea bag, David aimed to teach Michael valuable leadership lessons. This story sets the stage for exploring ten leadership lessons drawn from the humble tea bag, emphasizing humility, teamwork, and the importance of staying grounded. These lessons, illustrated through David and Michael's experiences, offer insights applicable to anyone striving to become a better leader and person.

Chapter Three

After a deep conversation with Michael, David discovered that Michael's team had the knowledge and experience needed for success, but their output was lacking due to poor team spirit. Michael, relying heavily on his prestigious business school background, felt superior and believed his team members were less knowledgeable. His constant rebukes during morning meetings demotivated his team, leading to a decline in performance. In contrast, David's team thrived because he appreciated their efforts, encouraged initiative, and fostered a positive environment. He believed in recognizing successes publicly and addressing issues privately, which boosted team morale and productivity.

David wanted Michael to understand his shortcomings and how improving his approach could enhance performance. Using the metaphor of a tea bag, David taught Michael that what matters is what's inside—the quality of the tea, not the packaging. Similarly, in leadership, it's not about titles, education, or outward appearances but about one's core values and attitude. Michael realized his mistake of valuing his MBA degree over the team's collective effort and the importance of maintaining a humble and supportive leadership style.

Michael acknowledged that his arrogance and lack of appreciation for his team were detrimental. Inspired by David's success, he saw the importance of motivating his team, treating everyone equally, and being approachable. David's leadership, characterized by humility and a team-caring attitude, resulted in high team morale and consistent success. The lesson is clear: true leadership is about who we are at our core and the values we uphold. By focusing on being good human beings and supporting our teams, we can achieve better results and foster a harmonious work environment.

Chapter Four

During a deeper conversation, David learned that Michael often avoided challenging assignments given by his Country Head. Michael preferred to stick to his defined responsibilities and avoid any extra tasks. One incident highlighted this behavior: the Country Head asked Michael to prepare a detailed report on peer companies' digital infrastructure and implement the best practices within 90 days. Although this task was slightly outside Michael's usual duties, it was critical and time-sensitive. Instead of embracing the challenge, Michael declined, fearing failure. This reaction disappointed his Country Head and explained Michael's poor annual appraisals.

David used this revelation to teach Michael a crucial lesson: "The real flavor emerges when the tea bag meets hot water." This metaphor means that just as a tea bag's true flavor is released in hot water, a person's true abilities are revealed in challenging situations. Comfort and ease don't showcase a leader's strengths; adversity does. Good leaders embrace tough times as opportunities to prove their worth. David encouraged Michael to see challenges as chances to demonstrate his leadership qualities rather than shy away from them.

Michael had an "aha" moment, realizing he missed an opportunity to prove himself as a true leader. He understood that he could have accepted the challenge, delegated tasks to his team, and guided the project to success. In the corporate world, leadership qualities, not just knowledge, are what lead to success and recognition. This lesson from the tea bag applies universally: to be a leader, you must embrace challenges and let your true capabilities shine.

Chapter Five

During a deep discussion, David realized that Michael's team lacked motivation and did not take the initiative unless explicitly directed. There was no team spirit or sense of belonging. Michael's leadership style was unapproachable, leading to a lack of guidance and support. As a result, the team felt isolated and unmotivated, contributing to their poor performance. In contrast, David's team thrived because he was open, approachable, and regularly shared his knowledge and experiences. This fostered a collaborative environment where team members felt valued and encouraged to contribute, significantly boosting productivity.

David used the metaphor of a tea bag to teach Michael an important lesson about leadership. He explained that just as a tea bag needs to be porous to release its flavor, a leader must be open and receptive. This means being open to new ideas, feedback, and the experiences of others. By doing so, a leader can absorb wisdom from various sources and adapt to different situations, promoting personal growth and effective leadership. This openness helps leaders connect with their teams, understand their needs, and inspire them to achieve their best.

Michael had an "aha" moment, realizing his mistake of isolating himself and not providing the necessary support to his team. He understood that being closed off had limited his team's potential and caused delays in their projects. Michael learned that by being more open and supportive, he could instill confidence in his team, creating a cohesive and high-performing group. This lesson taught him that blending with his team and adopting a porous attitude would not only improve his leadership but also gain appreciation from his superiors and set a positive example for others.

Chapter Six

David and Michael's conversation revealed that Michael's autocratic leadership style stifled his team's creativity and potential. Michael saw his team merely as helpers to follow his orders, which hindered their ability to share ideas or innovate. David recognized this attitude was harmful to both Michael and his team. He explained to Michael that leadership isn't confined to a position at the top; true leaders can be found at every level of an organization.

Using the tea bag metaphor, David highlighted that a tea bag functions no matter where it is in the cup, just as leadership potential isn't limited by hierarchy. This eye-opening lesson made Michael realize his mistake. He understood that every team member has leadership qualities, and it's crucial to nurture and encourage these qualities to elevate the entire organization. Michael resolved to support his team better and recognize their contributions, fostering a positive and collaborative atmosphere.

Chapter Seven

Michael was very happy with the previous lessons as David's insights opened his mind, making him feel ready to excel in his organization. However, there were still more lessons to learn, and Michael was eager to hear them. David noticed that Michael was trying to handle all the work alone, committing to finishing projects by himself but failing to deliver. Overwhelmed by the workload, Michael's assumption that he could manage everything alone led to failure, causing both him and his organization to suffer. Despite needing support, Michael never involved his colleagues, aiming to be a one-man army. David saw this mindset as harmful and shared the lesson, "Sometimes, one teabag is just not enough."

David explained that just as a large pot of tea needs more than one teabag to make a strong beverage, big challenges in an organization often require more than one leader. Asking for help is not a sign of weakness but a sign of strength and self-confidence. This lesson was an eye-opener for Michael. He realized that his failure to seek help was the main reason for his struggles. Understanding this, Michael acknowledged that he should have approached his boss and colleagues for support, which would have led to success and appreciation for his leadership. This change in mindset was crucial for Michael's growth and the overall success of the organization.

Chapter Eight

Michael felt increasingly confident as he absorbed valuable lessons from his friend

David. Eager to improve, he humbly asked David if there were more lessons from the tea bag to learn. David was thrilled by Michael's enthusiasm and felt fulfilled knowing he was making a positive impact. As their conversation continued, David discovered that Michael's project needed expertise in areas like analytics, Management Information Systems, and Information Technology. Michael, wanting all the credit, feared that involving colleagues would undermine his recognition. This mindset led him to take full responsibility and avoid seeking help, which David saw as a recipe for disaster.

David explained that just as adding sugar and milk to tea enhances its flavor, leaders need to collaborate with colleagues who have complementary skills. Michael's attempt to handle the project alone resulted in delays and dissatisfaction among his team, as he worked round the clock, causing unnecessary stress. The project failed to progress as expected because Michael relied solely on his limited knowledge and didn't seek the necessary expertise from others. David emphasized that good leaders understand their limitations and seek help to achieve a well-rounded outcome.

The lesson was an eye-opener for Michael. He realized that seeking help from colleagues would have solved many problems, saved time, and reduced stress for both him and his team. This insight applies to all of us: as project leaders, we shouldn't bear all the burden alone. Involving experts from different domains ensures that the right inputs are in place and the project rollout is seamless, leading to successful outcomes and a more harmonious work environment.

Chapter Nine

Through their conversations, David noticed Michael's arrogance and tendency to do everything himself. David decided to share one final lesson from the tea bag metaphor to help Michael stay grounded. He explained that just as a tea bag has a string held by someone else, leaders must remember they are accountable to others. No matter how powerful a leader becomes, there are always stakeholders or higher authorities who can pull them out of their position. This realization helps prevent leaders from becoming autocratic and ensures they remain humble.

Michael understood the importance of this lesson. He learned that as a leader, his role is to guide the team and ensure the project's success without becoming possessive or authoritarian. Acting like the sole owner of a project can lead to negative consequences and potentially result in removal from the position. The key is to stay grounded, humble, and focused on contributing to the organization's success, recognizing that ultimate control lies with higher authorities. These insights helped Michael see the value of humility and accountability in leadership.

Chapter Ten

David wanted Michael to understand a crucial insight from the tea bag metaphor: a leader's primary goal should be to build a strong team, focusing less on themselves and more on their team's development. He explained that no one praises the tea bag itself but the quality of the tea it produces. Similarly, great leaders are remembered not for their individual brilliance but for the success and excellence of their teams.

Michael learned that leadership isn't about self-focus or boasting about personal achievements. Often, leaders forget that their success is due to their team's efforts, and they should shine the spotlight on their team's contributions. Just like people appreciate the tea and not the tea bag, successful projects are valued for the collective effort rather than the individual leader. A good leader recognizes and appreciates the people behind the scenes, which helps them grow within the organization. Leaders who demonstrate care and humility are the ones who get promoted and advance seamlessly up the corporate ladder.

Chapter Eleven

David wanted Michael to understand a crucial lesson: no one in an organization is indispensable. Every person, no matter how passionate, will eventually leave the project or the company. David explained that projects have distinct phases: setup, nurturing, and then producing results. Once a project is running smoothly, it becomes a routine activity, and it's time for the leader to move on. Leaders should share their knowledge and let others take over to keep the organization growing.

Using the tea bag metaphor, David emphasized that just as tea bags know when to leave the cup after brewing, leaders should know when to step aside. Overstaying and clinging to their role can hinder progress. Michael understood this clearly and felt relieved. Grateful for David's wisdom, he pledged to revive his project with a new approach.

Bonus Chapter of my published book "Grab Your Victory Hour"

The sweetest and most joyful period of a lifetime is childhood. Reminiscing on my childhood days with my elder brother who was two years older than me, we were forced to wake up at 4:30 A.M to memorize the subjects taught in the school. My father used an antique alarm clock to wake both of us up. At that time, we were in preschool. Gradually we grew with this morning routine of waking up early. As time went by, our college days began and now we are both working professionals. My elder brother is currently not a morning person, but I have maintained the habit of waking up in the morning. I appreciate the habit of waking up early imbibed in me.

Every parent desire to make their kids shine and get the best results in class and above that, rank first place in school. At that time, I found that I was forced to wake up, but then there was no clarity in my mind about what I was reading and what was getting inside my head. Instead, I would feel sleepy and maybe after a lapse of 45 minutes, my brain and mind would open and I could now read the chapters.

Some research says that morning is the best time for cramming and my father agreed with this. However, I also found that this sentence also has another meaning for my father. My father made doubly sure that we had not slept back and that we were busy reading the books. The sound of our cramming might have given him a sense of fulfilment that kids are learning and their morning hours are best utilized. My brother and I kept on realizing that we were only gainfully utilizing only one of the two hours from 4.30 A.M. to 6.30 A.M. for study, but we dare not say this to our father as he was a strict disciplinarian. This concept of waking up early in the morning led me to research on utilizing the morning's best waking hours. Everyone desires to dream big and achieve their goals like wealth, peak of their career, wisdom, etc. And so was my dream. But the question is how many of us can connect and achieve the goal of our choice? We all have immense potential to achieve whatever we want in life.

In Swami Vivekananda's words, human souls have infinite potential and can achieve anything. This statement is true but requires wings and a burning desire to achieve what we need to accomplish in life. I have come across many people in my life who were students, professionals, and teachers. I observed that every personality I have interacted with has its routines. Some studying late at night and some waking up early in the morning but then they feel sleepy and inactive the entire day. They were missing the day's power pack. They want to change their habits but somehow, they can't. After much of my research on morning waking habits, listening to many podcasts, and reading several books, I concluded that the best way to utilize the morning after waking is first to CHARGE ONESELF WITH A SEQUENCE OF MORNING RITUALS. These morning rituals takes about 60 minutes, and I call this time "Victory Hour".

I have experimented with a series of morning rituals to energize me for the entire day and give me a new outlook for my journey towards becoming an extraordinary person. With my deep learning of morning habits, I desire to write about the morning rituals so that my readers can claim their 'victory hour' and utilize the hour as the best way to charge themselves for the entire day, making them more productive in their work.

How Did I Come About the Morning Rituals?

I was not getting a proper solution to use my morning time efficiently. I was confused as to what time I should wake up. How many hours of sleep I should mandatorily take? If I slept fewer hours, I felt that waking up at the ring of the alarm clock would not freshen up my mind as my body did not get the required hours of sleep. I would snooze my alarm clock button and go back to sleep. Later on, after waking up, I would realize that I had wasted my day again. Further to my frustration of not waking up, I also felt guilty for not sticking to my routine which I had prepared a day before. These routines included walking, reading books, meditating, etc. My thoughts and plan remained on paper, which happened most of the time. It was giving me set back day by day. Still, I was curious to find the real technique of utilizing one hour after waking up in the morning so that I can take on any activity for the entire day. As you read this book, I am sure you will also be going through the same phase, and this happens not only to you but to most of the people who want to become morning people but cannot achieve their goals. I congratulate you for purchasing this book as I can assure you that this dilemma will now be over once and for all. You have purchased this book and reached up to this page, which proves that you want to change your lifestyle and achieve the dreams of your choice. I was always looking for a solution to improve my lifestyle, inculcate good waking habits and utilize the morning hours most beneficially. I had always wanted to be a morning person who ritually sticks to waking up early and feeling energized for the entire day. There was a fire within me to best utilize the morning hours and maintain the consistency of my early waking-up habit. I have researched many books on morning habits to make morning waking a daily ritual. Some books talked about the activities you prefer to be done in the morning based on your liking which may be meditating, reading books, listening to soothing music, running, walking etc. But I was not getting the solution I wanted to kickstart my day. I read many books, listened to many Ted talks on morning habits, and finally, I could merge various concepts after experimenting with various permutations and combinations on me to form a set of morning habits that changed my life. I have been following these morning rituals for the past five years, and I strongly recommend adopting these rituals, which have changed my life.

I have devised strategic time-bound morning activities one after the other for 60 minutes that set the tone for the day. The activities re-energize and revitalize me and make me feel at the top of the world. After my morning activities, I feel highly confident, with all thoughts aligned properly for the entire day. My face gets a radiance with a positive outlook, and I am ready to accept any task for the day. My memory power and my intelligence to grab any subject have improved. In this journey, I have also treasured the secret of learning conceptually any subject which may be strange to me. I will reveal the secret to the entire universe in my next book, which on practicing, will lead you to become a learned personality in any subject, a personality which you have never imagined. Yes, I can vouch that the secret is that strong. But to achieve that, you must first become a morning person by practicing the techniques taught in this book. I want my readers to achieve their first level of success. I guarantee that you will be a changed person and achieve health, wealth, prosperity, and happiness. I have done it and achieved it, and still, I am achieving more.

The first principle to start the journey is to forget about your past, who you were, and what you did earlier. Every day is a new day, and it starts today. The book "Awaken the Giant Inside," by Anthony Robbins says that you are what you decide now and can transform yourself. The only mantra is to take a "Decision" and then see the changes this decision will bring in your life. People are in the habit of procrastinating, pulling themselves down, and slowly losing their self-confidence. They don't take decisions, and if they do, they don't remain firm. The first key to success is taking decisions, followed by the habit you must stick to in order to witness the fruits of the decision. Research tells us that if any activity is performed for a continuous 21 days, it becomes a habit, and eventually, after 21 days, one starts enjoying the new habit. I guarantee that once you cross 21 days, you cannot live without those habits. I will discuss in the chapters the morning rituals based on habits you must follow for 21 days. After 21 days, you can find the difference. You will be amazed to find yourself improving in all areas in whichever phase of life you are, whether you are a student, a professional, homemaker, a businessperson etc. This morning ritual is for everyone, and one can easily imbibe it and get a transformed life. You know what? Life is beautiful, and we should enjoy life by taking advantage of the full potential of mind and body. Once you control your mind and body, you can achieve anything extraordinary. So, let's start learning. A learning journey that is going to transform your life forever. Whatever techniques I am going to talk about are not only the techniques I have assimilated from various sources but also, I have experienced them. I will tell you about each technique in detail in the subsequent chapters. I have applied those techniques to myself and found a dramatic change within me. First and foremost, start with your sleeping habits.

How much sleep is required?

I have researched several articles on the optimum hours of sleep required, but I could not find the answer. Based on the various articles I have read, I did multiple experiments on myself by sleeping early and resting for 7 hours, 8 hours and even for 9 hours. Sleeping to what extent is important is always a question in the mind of everyone. I am sure these thoughts might be going through your thought process as well as how many hours to sleep because many times if you sleep late, you do not feel fresh in the morning. The entire day you feel lazy. But the question is whether this is a roadblock in our minds. Whether our mind should witness 7 or 8 hrs of sleep and only then we can feel fresh in the morning. You will not agree with me now. Once you go through the chapters you will understand the science of feeling energetic. I have interacted with many people and asked how many hours of sleep they need. I get the answer in the range of 7hrs-8hrs, and some even say 9 hrs. But when I ask them, do you feel fresh after waking up? I get a mixed reply. Some say yes, and some say it depends on sleep quality. But then I also ask them if they feel energetic the whole day and have good vibes and thoughts for performing their work in the office or business. Few are sure, but few are unsure of where their life is taking them. They are just flowing wherever life takes them. In the book "Awaken the Giant Inside", Anthony Robbins said that for most people, their life is like a free boat moving in the direction of a stream of water. Wherever the stream is taking the boat, the boat is moving, but at one point, when the sudden steep creeks come, the boat goes along with the water flow and falls into the creek. This is dangerous. Similarly, people take their lives. Their lives move like the boat moving with the flow of a stream. They don't take charge of their life of which they are capable. They can change the direction of their life with just one decision to change their life for the better like using the oars. The direction of the boat can be changed, and the boat can be moved to a pleasant place where one can see more greenery and enjoy the surroundings. This example calls for immediate taking control of our life, and each of us can do it.

Life is wonderful, but the only essential is to know the technique of enjoying life. I will tell you how to enjoy life and take full advantage of life. Each one of the readers here is blessed to have a beautiful life. Life of your dreams. A life on your terms. A life of financial freedom. A life of abundance and wealth. A life of good health, and I guarantee that once you follow the techniques given in the book- you will be amazed to find a dramatic improvement in yourself. Yes, you can and have the inherent potential to do that. All the techniques I will discuss in this book are straightforward and do not require spending any amount. It is simply maintaining consistency in your morning ritual habits that you must perform in your Victory Hour. The only commitment I want from you is to follow the Morning Victory Hour habits in true spirit and not miss a day practicing those techniques.

Some readers may think they are night owls and can't wake up in the morning. They have been sleeping very late in the night for so many years and will find it hard to suddenly break that chronic habit. The answer is you can with just one decision of waking up early in the morning no matter when you sleep. It is a hard decision, but it will bring you positive results. The following quote of Boxing Champion Muhammad Ali will inspire you **"I hated every minute of training, but I said," Don't quit. Suffer now and live the rest of your life as a champion."**

One should always take a cue from the universe to lead a beautiful life. The way the universe operates for the entire 24 hours from the rising sun to sunset to night. Similarly, our body is made on certain principles and follows the universe's clock. The universe, if you observe minutely, teaches us a lot. The rising of the sun and the setting of the sun have a fixed time. When the sun rises, a beautiful morning starts with sun rays becoming brighter and brighter, and all living beings are expected to start their day and get busy in their activities. After sunset, the sun's rays slowly dimmer, and the same bright day becomes dark, indicating that living beings should start settling for rest and sleep. Universe has set the timetable of daytime for work and night for sleeping. This is the first principle on which the learnings of this book are based. Some readers might think that because of their office work they have to work late at night and then how do they wake up in the morning? Don't worry. This book is for everyone, and the techniques taught do not impress upon seven or eight hours of sleep. It teaches you to energize yourself for the whole day by practicing the laid-down techniques after you wake up. You must "Grab your victory hour" after you wake up and follow the rituals taught in the book to become more productive in your work, achieve your dreams, and succeed in any field you desire. You become extraordinary by practicing the techniques for 60 minutes daily. Enjoy your learning journey.

Scan the QR Code to read more

Bonus Chapter of my published book "Wake Up Your Sleeping Giant"

Because of the umpteen pressure in today's hectic lifestyle, we all are in the whirlpool of just leading the life where life is taking us. At this juncture, you as a professional will be in a sales job, marketing job, administrative job, MNC executive, Corporate CEO etc. You are doing what is necessary, but you cannot find the time for yourself which you want, but somehow life comes in between, and you have to drop the idea which you think can change your well-being as well. You are not alone in this universe facing such an issue of balancing life and work. Many professionals are facing this issue. This is the problem statement, and the generations are passing through this problem. You are facing this problem, but you feel helpless to change your life and lifestyle and give time to your family. Don't you? This book will try to solve all your problems, and you will be a changed personality after reading this book. You will discover in this book a hidden giant sleeping inside you, just waiting for your direction to activate and do wonders for you. You have infinite potential which you are not aware of. This will be revealed to you in the later chapters. Everyone in this universe has problems, whether he is a company CEO, a multi-billionaire, a working professional, or any human being. Yes, the problem exists with everyone, but he is successful and knows how to cope with the problem. How to come victorious of that problem. Does this require a mindset change? Whether you have a fixed mindset or a growth mindset? You don't know, but while reading through the chapters, you will get to know the truth behind the different mindsets and how you can cultivate a growth mindset which can give a different lens of the problem you are going through. Are you a professional who is aspiring for promotion in your job? Are you a professional who wants to have more energy to guide your team? Are you a professional who cannot meet the sales target and wants to meet the target? Are you a professional who wants to climb up the corporate ladder much faster than your colleagues? As a top management professional of your organization, are you lacking the energy to convince for joint ventures? The problems are many, but in essence, these are not the problems but the lack of tightening of the nuts and bolts of the brain. Yes, what I am claiming is true! These are not all the problems, but the result of the fixed mindset, which to date you have not changed but nothing to worry about as now you are in the right hand. Your book in your hand will mentor you to change yourself and bring all success you deserve. The principles talked about in the book will bring you laurels in your life. After reading this book, you will be a changed personality. You will change completely, and good fortunes will come to you. Many a time, we feel that we don't have time. But is it so? Then why are so many successful personalities in any field you take? I will not name them which you know better, but have you ever thought why they are successful and Billionaire? It's not that they have more than 24 hours in a day. They are also equally capable like you, but they are different today. Why? There must be some secrets they are following that you are unaware of. I will walk you through all those secrets which a successful person follows. There is one formula: "If anyone can do it successfully, you too can do it". Success always leaves clues, and you need to follow those clues to become the same successful person. As I will reveal in the chapters, you have infinite potential, and only a spark is needed to ignite that sleeping giant within yourself. I will reveal all the clues of the successful people which will make you another successful personality that the world will discuss. Then it will become your moral responsibility to propagate the wisdom you will read in this book. There is a Burning Desire within you to do something different; therefore, you are reading this book, and I can vouch that this first step of yours will lead you to cross the bridge, leading to good fortune. Research shows that (FBC)- faith, burning desire, and consistency- will move the mountains. Roger Bannister, an athlete with a clear vision of becoming the best runner in the world by setting a record of running one mile in under four minutes, had faith in his vision. He continuously dreamt of running one mile in less than four minutes. This was humanly impossible, and many doctors in the town said it was impossible for a human being to run 1 mile in 4 minutes. But it was the sheer determination of Roger Bannister to create the record. He dreamt of his victory; he practised intensely. Every day he woke up at 4 am and practised. In his mind, there was no other thought but to win the milestone. The entire Universe is the witness to what happened on May 6th, 1954. Roger Bannister broke the world record, and to the surprise of all the doctors in the town, he achieved the record of running 1 mile in 3 minutes and 54 seconds. How was this possible? Was it something unnatural? Was it something extraordinary? Yes, Roger Bannister's determination to succeed was the first stepping stone to his success. He believed in his belief to stand victorious and achieve the world record. He developed a burning desire to achieve the milestone he had seen in his mind, and his consistency in practice daily brought laurels to him. He got many accolades. The entire Universe congratulated him. Some even told him that he was lucky. But the harsh reality only Roger knows. His success was not a single-day success but a consistent and persistent effort. It was his dedicated and consistent effort to wake up every morning at 4 am and start practising. Think about the same situation in your life. You are also like Rogger Banister in your field. You can achieve anything in your career if you are determined to achieve that. Today as a working professional, you might have targets to meet, and you find it difficult and uncomfortable to attend presentations for business review. You are being questioned about the business gap. You have only answered, "Definitely, in the coming quarter or the next month, you will achieve the target". But again, the same situation arises. In the next business review meeting, you face the same situation of the percentage gap in the business figures you were supposed to meet, and you have also committed to achieving that. Still, you were not able to achieve it. Whereas some of your colleagues can achieve the target and get good remarks from the top management in the review meeting. What makes the difference between you and him? For example, if you are a sales professional, you may say that your counterpart's territory has more potential, his products are more demanding in that territory and so on. Similar is true for the Head of the Corporate Verticals. Some Vertical Heads can attract good reviews in the business conference meeting, whereas others get direction to improve further. Why does this happen? When teams are aligned for the vertical heads to assist him in his job, why is one vertical head always a blue-eyed boy of the top management and others are not? There must be some game-changer rules which the other person is following and that you are not following. But don't worry. This book is deep research of the successful person's various activities, which the author has vetted. Yes, the practices in this book have been experimented by me, and I have found a sea change in my personality and well-being. I am continuing the journey and assure you that if you follow and practice the principles in the book, you will be a changed personality with many successful vibes. **You will realize the hidden potential within you which was sleeping till now,** and I call this hidden potential your

"SLEEPING GIANT". This book has been written with a lot of masterpieces and research work. It is the second in the series of the earlier book published by the author, "Grab your Victory Hour", which has been widely appreciated by readers for bringing a change in their life and personality.

The first chapter of this book, "Wake up your Sleeping Giant", talks about the "The Power of Morning Hour", where you will realize how beautiful is the morning hours and how you have missed all these days not utilizing the benefit of those golden hours which can set the tone of the day for you.

The second chapter talks about "Setting the stage for success and preparing you for the morning routine", as facts will be revealed to you about how to utilize the morning hour and make yourself ready for the aggressive fight for the day and which in turn will make you look aggressive in your work. You will progress much faster in your professional career.

The third Chapter talks about "Mindset Matters: How you start your day with a positive attitude" and gives insights into eight morning rituals that will completely transform you. It guarantees you mental and physical energy, which will help you take complete charge of the day. You will rise on the Corporate Ladder with the mental energy you generate.

The fourth chapter discusses "Productivity Hacks: Maximizing your time and efficiency" and reveals the secret to maximizing your time and efficiency in your work. You will learn how efficiently you can concentrate on your work, which will give you immense satisfaction.

The Fifth Chapter talks about "Planning and Prioritization: Organizing your tasks and goals" and how these two Ps are essential to achieving victory in your life and achieving any target, whether be Sales, Marketing, administrative skills, business ventures etc. In this chapter, you will learn about the application of important principles in your work, which will make a much difference in the style of functioning you have been following till now.

This book promises to awaken the sleeping giant within you and bring you a changed personality with loads of success and good fortunes. This book is for working professionals who want to streamline their work at the office, want to make progress in their career, and quickly climb up the corporate ladder.

Scan QR code to read more

Bonus Chapter of my published book

"5 Minutes of Daily Visualization"

People say that one should not look back on life; life is meant to move forward. This is very true; I am also a true believer of this idea. Everyone in his life will experience ups and downs; life is meant to be like that. It is like the graphical representation of a heartbeat, which is a curved line moving up, then down, and then moving up.

The curve becomes straight only when there is no life. So, for life to exist, the curve of the circumstances of our life must be both up and down. We may never have explored that the curve of the circumstances of life are always on an upward path. If I say this, I will contradict what has been said for ages: man is governed by destiny.

I used to entertain this notion, but now I totally deny it. I was told since childhood that every human being in this universe has a limitation. One is bound by destiny: you will achieve anything great in life only if it is your fate. God has carved a specific future for everyone; and it's true for me as well. Although my parents always encouraged me to do my best and achieve the most in life, we all know that our thoughts and beliefs are the average of the five people surrounding us.

My parents told me that there is no such term as fate, but the words of friends and relatives affect our minds. Now I believe that I am the victim of fabricated beliefs. In my schooling days, some students used to get high marks and earn top rank in class. They enjoyed the blessings of the teachers. In every subject, these so-called bright students used to score the higher marks and would earn great appreciation from the school community.

In fact, the best students' photographs would be published in the school magazine, which was published quarterly. My photograph was never published in the school magazine, so I grew up with the belief that I was a mediocre student. With every passing day, my belief got stronger and stronger. I felt myself being pushed back.

Life is like the sea; it will keep you near the shore with its waves if you are not strong enough to venture farther in. If your belief is not strong, you will not give yourself over to the circumstances. Just like the waves of water pushing you out to sea, you will find yourself out of the race of life. Writing these lines has brought tears to my eyes. I realize that all the beliefs about myself were my own created thoughts.

I kept on diminishing myself; with each passing day and the glory of my classmates who stood first, second, and third in class, I started comparing myself to the brightest students of the class. I started developing the belief that these students were more outspoken with the teachers, and they were the first to solve any questions on any subject.

These thoughts became true in the end. I felt neglected seeing how the teachers appreciated those students for solving the questions first. Today, when I look back, I laugh at myself. With negative thoughts, I made myself small. Why did this happen? Let me tell you. As two brothers, both of us gained admission to different schools for kindergarten. When I was admitted, I was very excited to join the school. In fact, I found a good bunch of friends to play with on the first day of admission. I was joyous on the inside, and my teachers liked my innocence. I got good attention in school. My teachers gave me the proper handholding.

I vividly remember that the teachers proactively helped me. They developed a lot of interest in me, and I felt motivated because of it. Most of the time, I would raise my hand to answer questions first. The teachers started to acknowledge my proactive attitude, and they appreciated me. Many a time, I set as an example for the other students. Being the first to finish the classwork, I earned the opportunity to be the class monitor. To designate a student as monitor was an "incentive tool" that teachers would use to motivate the students.

This kept me on cloud nine; the aftereffect was that I became the pride of my parents. I remember that my father was called to hoist flag at school while I stood by, first in the class. I clearly remember his face: his son had made him proud. Being a guest at the flag hoisting ceremony was a proud moment for my father. These activities gave me confidence in school as well as at home. I became the darling of my teacher, even though I was notorious — something I will reveal in upcoming lines.

At home, I could flawlessly execute my homework. I would only need a little guidance from my father. Every day was a bright one for me as I continued to enjoy the company of my friends. In a very short span of time, I became their leader; they followed me in any activity I chose. I had a few gangs of my best buddies; they were always with me during recess and sports. In simple words, I used to enjoy myself a lot; today I can very well say that those were my "Golden Days".

I was in this school until grade three. There was a reason. As two brothers, the elder was studying in a different school in a five-days-a-week program. However, my school was six days a week. Because of this, Father made the decision to admit me to my brother's school eventually to have a good family life, where the whole family could enjoy the weekend together.

It was a very good move on my father's part. Had I been in his place, I would have also done the same thing for my kids. But being a child — the blue-eyed boy of the teachers and the leader of my best buddies — I felt a shock. I thought that my created nest was going to be destroyed. Feelings of sadness started cropping up. I did not want to leave my friends and nor did my friends want to leave my company. I clearly remember the day when I broke the news that I would have to leave the school to go to my brother's school; all my friends were upset.

Suddenly, there was silence among my friends, and everyone felt sad. Yes, they had every reason for their less than sanguine feelings because they felt their leader, their jolly friend, would be leaving them. I recall that every day during recess period, as friends, we would share snacks prepared by our mothers. We could taste various foods, and the joy of sharing was enormous. I remember when my father came to pick me up from school one day; all my fellow friends encircled him and kept firing questions as to why he was taking their friend out of school. They literally pleaded with Father to take back his decision of getting me admitted in another school.

Those all friends were innocent kids; they could not see the bigger picture...the one my father had seen for me. People used to say that my brother's school was one of the best in the locality. Getting admission there was tough, and many students had great success after leaving. But life had to move forward, and Father filled out the admission form for class three in my brother's school.

My father was called for an interview. The funniest part came on the day of interview; I still remember it. I am sure you will laugh at my innocence. It so happened that when my turn came, there was a bell sound from the principal's office and an errand boy approached us. He asked Father to bring me in. I was eating chocolate, relishing the melodious taste in the core of my heart. But there came a sudden disruption to my joy. I was forced to wrap the chocolate and keep it in its bag before proceeding for the interview. This made me upset; I didn't want to miss the moment of enjoying the taste of chocolate.

I followed orders, and we went into the principal's room. I remember that the principal was wearing white attire; he had a beautiful smile on his face when we entered. He welcomed me and asked a few simple questions like the spelling of "aeroplane", "elephant", etc. Now listen to what I did: I did not utter a word and just looked here and there. I kept my face blank. Father kept observing me, with the hope that I would answer as he had taught me several times. But my mind was fixed on the chocolate; so,

I did not utter a word. The feeling of losing my best friends was also on my mind. The principal kept watching me, hoping to hear the right answer from my mouth. But a deep silence reigned. He waited 10 minutes for me to respond, but lost hope and asked my father to take his child away.

My father with a heavy heart walked out of the room; as expected, his face was red with anger. He asked me why I did not answer the questions, which he had taught me several times. My innocent answer brought a different smile to his face. I didn't know what was going on inside his mind. My answer was, "Why you did not allow me to eat chocolate; because of that, I was sad and angry".

Oh, God what a foolish thing I did. I have a reason for sharing my childhood stories. I want to relate with the power of visualization what I am going to talk about in the next chapter. In fact, I want to set the context so you can walk with me on this journey of visualization. Back to the story: that year I did not get admission to my brother's school. Hearing the news was an exuberant moment for my friends. I felt the same and continued my journey with friends, as usual.

This golden period continued for one year. By this time, I had completed class three in my school happily with my friends. For class four, my father again filled out the form; he was adamant to get me admitted into my brother's school. This time, he left no stones unturned in my preparation for the interview. I had also matured. I did well in the interview. I was successful, and my name was displayed on the school noticeboard for selection to class four. Father was very happy; he immediately took the certificate from my present school.

It was a shock for my friends, but life had to move on. I started a new life in my new school. I found a difference in the syllabus and the way the teachers instructed the students. There were definitely more books to read and more home assignments. Somehow, I felt that things were moving very fast; I was just going with the flow. I was not able to capture the concepts. Everything was moving very fast. School ran from 8 am to 2 pm. I reached home every day at around 3 pm. In the afternoon, I was asked to take a nap for one hour and then study for one hour. I tried to concentrate, but many of the concepts taught in the school were not very clear to me. When I tried to understand, there was a burden in my mind to complete the home assignments.

Somehow, I was not able to gel with the school. On the examinations, I could score marks but not on a par with the few students who earned good marks. I was no longer the blue-eyed boy of the teachers as in the previous school. My confidence went down with each passing day. I started developing the belief of being a mediocre student. I wanted to make a U-turn. What I want to impart is that our belief system is based on the circumstances we pass through. If you view my background, you will note that I was a bright student in my previous school. I would have been a topper. My confidence level would have been very high. My belief would have been as a bright student.

In the new school, gradually over a period of time, my belief shifted from a bright to a mediocre student. Today when I realized this, things look totally different. I have overcome my old belief with a new one, developed in ignorance and based on the circumstances I was going through. Today I am a successful person having scored a very good rank on many examinations at various levels. In my organization, my work is appreciated. I have also received the tag of "best employee".

Going forward and giving you a glimpse of my present life — where technology has made life very easy and this world very small — it is very easy to get connected with school friends; in fact, all our friends are on social media platforms. We communicate at intervals; when I compare their success with mine, I find myself above them. In my organization, I lead a team of one hundred people; it is a dream for many of my friends to reach that cadre. I have all the needed facilities, from a chauffeur-driven car to an expensive flat with all amenities. I live in the financial capital Mumbai.

I have written in my previous book, "Wake Up Your Sleeping Giant" that morning rituals have been a pure transformer of my life. I have been practicing the eight morning rituals every morning for sixty minutes for the last five years, and it has totally transformed me. I can say this with pride. You too can change yourself if you remain committed to your morning habits. If you have not read my previous book, please do read it. It is a game changer.

To conclude this chapter, I would like to say that my belief of being a mediocre student developed because I started accepting the circumstances in front of me. I did not question why I am not able to understand school subjects well. I did not question why I was doing so well in my previous school and what was suddenly happening in the new one. I had the same intelligence; what had changed was only the circumstance. My school had been changed, my friends got changed, and my teachers got changed. The rest was as usual. Whether my mind did not accept the change, or I did not want to change, I didn't know.

In my subconscious mind, I might not have accepted the new environment. I wanted to go back to my previous school. Life is like this; every one of us has passed through such situations in some way or another. What is required is to accept the truth — the circumstances in which we find ourselves — and see life from a new perspective. The only thing that changes is change". So, embrace it and look for the positivity in it.

Try to explore the new life God has brought to you. Even the cocoon breaks out and becomes a beautiful larva. It struggles to come out and find itself in a new environment — a totally different environment. But with the struggle and the passage of the time, it becomes a beautiful butterfly to be appreciated by everyone. The butterfly becomes a part of nature. It gets totally transformed. The same is true for all of us. If I relate to my school journey, once again, I should have tried to approach my teachers to clear my doubts. I should have taken the pains to reach these teachers during recess and ask them to explain the misunderstood concepts. They would have felt good to see a student come forward like that.

At home, I should have discussed my circumstances with my parents. I could have used their help to make my study concepts clearer. I could have sought out my elder brother for more understanding. I could have practiced more assignments at home and generated questions for the next day to ask my teachers. But instead, I was overwhelmed with the new environment and never asked anything. I simply accepted the circumstances and got pushed back in the race of life. I mentally accepted that I was not able to win against those bright students in the class. This belief was strengthened day by day. I accepted that whatever was happening was truth, and it was my fate.

Now when I look back, I find myself laughing at what I did. Later in upcoming chapters, I will discuss the functions of the mind — specific to the conscious and subconscious mind. You will be shocked to learn the power of the subconscious mind. How your thoughts work and how you attract circumstances in your life will be discussed in detail. I have purposefully narrated my story to make you see that belief is the first seed we plant in our minds; this belief has a limiting character that results in our actions determined by the experiences around us.

In the next chapter, I will cover the belief system. Belief is the foundation of life; and once you are fully able to understand the law of belief, you can take your life to the next level. I have done so in my life. I have had many successes which I will reveal when I get an opportunity to talk to you. Now let's move on and get in-depth knowledge on how a belief system affects our lives.

Scan QR code to read more

May I ask you a small favor

I value your thoughts and feedback on this book immensely. I'm open to hearing all perspectives, whether positive or critical, as your input is crucial for refining and improving future editions. Please feel free to share your comments or concerns by emailing me at gyansnarayan22@gmail.com. I look forward to your insights.

If you enjoyed the book, please consider leaving a review. Your feedback not only supports my work but also helps others discover ways to become more productive. Thank you for reading and for being part of this journey!

Acknowledgement

I thank my parents, who have inculcated in me a good habit of reading books, making this book compilation possible for you. I am highly indebted to my wife, Sanchita, who always encouraged me to write the learnings I practice by listening to various podcasts and reading self-help books for the betterment of the readers. This book would not have been possible without her support and the sacrifices she made at weekends allowing me to write the book in solitude. I would also like to acknowledge the sacrifice made by my little daughter, Ishanvi, as she did not demand to play with me whenever she found me writing the manuscript. I love both of them.

Copyright

Copyright © 2024 by Gyan S Narayan. All rights reserved. No part of this book may be reproduced in any form without permission in writing from the author. No part of this publication may be reproduced or transmitted in any form or by any means, mechanical or electronic, including photocopying or recording, or by any information storage and retrieval system, or transmitted by email or by any other means whatsoever without permission in writing from the author.

Reference

The Secret of Leadership by Prakash Iyer

Disclaimer

The information given in this book is based on the research done by the author and the opinion expressed in the book are of author in his individual capacity and does not represent any institution in any manner. All content, including text, graphics, images and information contained on or available through this book is for general information purposes only.

www.ingramcontent.com/pod-product-compliance
Lightning Source LLC
Chambersburg PA
CBHW071829210526
45479CB00001B/59